Details

Details

How To Design with Architectural Salvage and Antiques

Brian D. Coleman

with photography by Dan Mayers

Gibbs Smith, Publisher
Salt Lake City

First Edition
10 09 08 07 06   5 4 3 2 1

Published by
Gibbs Smith, Publisher
P.O. Box 667
Layton, UT 84041

www.gibbs-smith.com
Orders: 1.800.748.5439

Designed by FORTHGEAR
Printed and bound in Hong Kong

Library of Congress Cataloging-in-Publication Data

Coleman, Brian D.
Details: how to design with architectural salvage and antiques/Brian D.
Coleman; with photographs by Dan Mayers. – 1st ed.
     p. cm.
ISBN 1-58685-523-9
1. Decoration and ornament, Architectural, in interior decoration.
2. Antiques in interior decoration. 3. Building materials–Recycling.
4. Building fittings–Recycling. I. Title.

NK2115.5.A73C64 2006
747–dc22

2005025782

Contents

Introduction

Details are what make the difference, and nowhere is this more important than in home construction and design. More and more homeowners are discovering architectural salvage as a way to add interest to their homes, to make them more compelling and unique.

Whether it's the well-worn, chipped-paint charm of a section of Victorian wrought-iron railing recast as a fireplace screen, or an old soapstone sink given a new lease on life in a kitchen, architectural salvage packs a punch that is hard to beat. In *Extraordinary Details: Decorating with Architectural Salvage and Antiques*, we looked at homes that used architectural salvage in creative and inspiring ways. In this book we explore how to use architectural salvage in more detail and, in the process, provide answers to many common questions, such as, "How do I use an old stained glass window that isn't the right size?" or "What exactly is the right type of mantel for my home?" Front door hardware, vintage lighting, mantels, sinks, stairs and staircases, and stained glass windows are types of salvage we will examine.

The message for using salvage is simple: don't be afraid if it's not perfect. Remember, there's nothing wrong with something that has a few nicks and scrapes—they only add to the charm. A minor crack in a window can often be stabilized, an uneven and askew window frame realigned or a missing knob replaced. Many prefer imperfections, in fact, as they add a patina of time that is hard to reproduce. Think twice about repainting that old door or window—its crusty, peeling paint has a beauty of its own you'll never be able to match. Of course, not all of us go so far as the homeowner who distressed his pine kitchen doors with a hammer and chain before their installation to ensure they would blend in appropriately with the time-worn texture of his antique kitchen cabinets!

Using architectural salvage need not be complicated. Try decorating with salvage for a quick and easy way to give your home a fresh and individual look. One enterprising apartment owner used flea market finds to redecorate his Manhattan apartment, including school maps from the 1930s that he recycled as window shades—and he even found a period light fixture of a globe to match. Or how about the homeowners who combined rusty iron newel posts with wooden spindles in their new home for instant vintage charm?

Knowledge is power, and the more you know and understand about salvage the easier it is to use. In *Details* we have gathered a forum of experts in the field to discuss architectural salvage in depth. Web Wilson, well-known author and antiques dealer in vintage hardware, examines the types of hardware used on both interior and exterior doors, from hinges and lock sets to pocket door rollers. Mary Ellen Polson, a well-respected author on interior design and editor at *Old House Interiors* magazine, surveys vintage lighting from Federal to Retro (1960s–70s) with good pointers and tips on their use. Mantels, the focal point of any room, are discussed in detail by Dan Cooper, a knowledgeable and frequent contributing writer for *Old House Interiors*. Jill Wilson, well-known antiques dealer and designer, discusses sinks, something everyone undergoing restoration of a kitchen or bath should be familiar with. Polson again contributes advice on stairs and staircases, taking the mystery and confusion out of them. And I discuss the secrets of incorporating stained glass into your home, which isn't that secret after all.

Salvaged school maps from the 1930s and a globe light fixture decorate a Manhattan apartment.

Details is meant to be a source of ideas and inspiration. No matter what type of home you live in, whether it's a suburban bungalow or an urban high-rise apartment, don't be afraid of architectural salvage. It's easy and enjoyable to add to your home, and with a little knowledge, not all that difficult to incorporate into your décor. You'll find it is one of the most satisfying and simple ways to give your interiors unique character and charm.

Old moldings and a salvaged mirror are transformed into a hall tree in this Manhattan apartment.

Fine Finishing Touches for Your Doors

The builders' hardware companies of the nineteenth century often referred to their products as "jewelry for the home," and once you begin to notice the beauty and usefulness of little architectural gems such as doorknobs, hinges, and keyhole escutcheons, you'll be bound to agree. Antique hardware often combines exquisite designs with imaginative details, and the American eclectic architecture of the late nineteenth century offered a myriad of opportunities to install these fine finishing touches in both common and uncommon places.

The most obvious place to find architectural hardware is, of course, on doors, and doorknobs are likely the first things you will see. But doorknobs are the last thing installed rather than the first, so start your hardware adventure by checking out the largest item you almost never see: the lock or latch set inside the edge of your door.

From the 1840s until the 1930s American carpenters installed mortise locks in just about every door they hung. These locks came in all sizes and were buried in the edge of the door so all that showed were thin front pieces that, during the decades of

Left: An Anglo-Japanese entryway lockset ca. 1870 graces the front door of this Victorian home.

Right: Pintel hinges have one leaf that slides onto a pin set in the other leaf. They must be installed right side up or the door will fall off.

ultra-fancy hardware, were often cast with fancy designs in high relief. You can uninstall a mortise lock by first removing the knobs and spindle and then the two screws on the front plate. It is noteworthy that most builders' hardware is not marked by the maker, except for mortise lock cases, and these are rarely seen. However, builders often bought locks and other hardware from several companies, so the knobs and doorplates may be from different makers.

Interior, or "passage," doors used mortise locks primarily for a latching function, although most could also be locked with a simple skeleton key. These locks take a 1/4-inch spindle and passage-size knobs that are 2-1/4 inches in diameter. At first, passage knobs were set into thin round "rosettes," which allowed the knob to turn without damaging the wood. Below the knob and rosette, a separate escutcheon

Above: Fancy little night works, with their matching rosettes, or back plates, allowed homeowners to easily open their front doors from the inside while the outside knob remained locked. This was made possible by using a split spindle—one of several mechanical issues that make it difficult to exchange or modify entrance-door hardware.

Right: Hinges ca. 1875 featuring Geisha girls and parasols reflect the Anglo-Japanese craze of the period.

Left: Late-nineteenth-century bronze hardware from France sets off the French doors.

Lower Left: Large, fancy keyhole escutcheons were used before development of the double keyhole mortise lock. These examples were cast in lead and then heavily plated with copper.

Lower Right: Fancy porcelain door trim was widely available and highly popular in the 1850s and 60s. Note how brass was used for the rosettes insert, the back plate for the keyhole escutcheon and also the doorknob shank.

Opposite Left: This large mortise cup escutcheon or pocket door pull in the American Aesthetic taste is just one of many pieces of the 1880 Japanese Suite offered by Russell & Erwin of New Britain, Connecticut.

plate was attached to cover the keyhole. By the mid-1870s, a rectangular doorplate that combined the rosette and keyhole became standard.

It is said that what is old becomes new again, and in the late 1830s, the first locks mortised into doors required a large hole to be drilled through the door stile and then two pre-set knob-and-spindle units were bolted together around a tube latch. Antique house owners of the twenty-first century will recognize this as "ye olde quick-set" doorknob system, which was reinvented about 1930 and has been standard in the United States since the 1950s. If your house has this often low-quality and unattractive hardware, up until recently it has been nearly impossible to swap it out because nothing will cover the 2-1/8-inch hole. Now, however, Old Rose Hardware of Portsmouth, Rhode Island, offers a special adaptor and authentic rosette designs that make it easy to install antique doorknobs on modern doors.

Many buildings of the nineteenth and early twentieth centuries had pairs of interior doors called sliders, or pocket doors, that required a very different hardware system. Each door held a mortise lock, but one had a curved latch tongue so it would enter the other lock and hold fast. If a pocket door was slid back into the wall, you pushed a button on the front of the lock, which in turn extended a little andle for pulling the door forward. Instead of doorknobs, each pocket door had a pair of "flush cup escutcheons," or pocket door pulls, that were mortised into the door stile. Usually a stubby little folding key stayed inside one escutcheon so it would be handy when needed.

Pocket doors ran on iron rollers buried in the wall and therefore did not need the other critical piece of

This knuckle-type hinge dates from the mid-1880s. Note the unusual combination of cast-iron leaves and the bronze pin tips.

hardware found on all other types of doors: hinges. Passage-door hinges were made from either iron or bronze and were often fancy-cast to complement the doorknobs and back plates. In the second and third quarters of the nineteenth century, pintel hinges, where one leaf drops onto a pin set permanently into the opposing leaf, were standard. Pintel hinges must be installed for the correct hand of the door, but fortunately, most are marked with an *L* or an *R* to help you make the correct choice.

As many old-house owners know, some interior doors are so large and heavy that three hinges are required. Such homes (usually of the 1845–75 vintage) often feature very heavy baseboard molding as well, and this requires the hinge to be properly offset to allow the door to swing open without interference. Hinges for such doors have about an inch of the backside of each leaf decorated like the face of the leaf because that much hinge will extend beyond the edge of the door when it is closed.

Somewhere around 1875, the knuckle-style hinge, with a removable pin that drops into the meshed knuckles, came to market. These hinges could be used for either right- or left-hand doors and quickly became the standard building product that is still used today. During the decades of Great American Hardware (1850–1900), many hinges were cast with the maker's name and the size; but remember, you can find hardware from various makers on the same door.

Exterior doors, and especially the main entry door, used very different hardware from passage doors. First of all, there was the critical issue of security, so mortise locks needed to be bigger and stronger and include a dead-bolt function. Until the late 1860s, most front doors had a small doorknob with a single keyhole below, but gradually the standard entry knob grew to 2-1/2 inches in diameter, and front-door

Below: This entry knob and doorplate graced a fine home built about 1885. Note the two keyholes and the swing cover. The two knobs with starburst designs show the difference between entry size and passage size.

Right: The heads of phoenixes adorn the door handles of these bookcases.

trim became one of the focal points of new-home construction. When compression-cast bronze hardware was developed around 1870, many companies offered exotic triangular rosettes and elaborate keyhole escutcheons that are prized by antique hardware collectors today.

By the early 1870s, homeowners were tired of throwing the deadbolt every time they came or went, and lock makers figured out how to design both a latch function and a security function in a single mortise case. Henceforth, front door locks had two keyways: one for the latchkey, which was used during the day, and a second for the master key, which set the deadbolt. On the exterior side of the front door, the master keyhole usually included a decorated swing cover.

The evolution of these double key locks is itself a fascinating study in American industrial design, as some early models featured keyways that were side by side rather than one above the other.

The interior side of later-nineteenth-century entry doors also used some special hardware. The doorknob was usually passage size, and often it was set into a rosette rather than a full-length plate. There would be a covered keyhole escutcheon for the master key and the latch keyway would be fitted with a little thumb turn, or "night works," that had its own miniature rose. Sometimes all three functions were combined into a single doorplate that lined up with the mechanics of the mortise lock.

All this variation means that replacing or trading out front-door hardware can be a challenge. If your mortise lock needs to be replaced, you'll have to find one that matches up with the keyways on your doorplates. Likewise, if you want to change the door trim, the new plates will have to match the lock openings. Also, take note that the size of the spindle used with entry locks is larger than for passage hardware. This means that the inside entry knob will have to accept the

large spindle size, and such knobs are not easy to find.

The spindle size for entry knobs has not changed from 5/16 inch, but, due to different mechanics, there are many variations on how it actually works the lock. Be sure to carefully look over your front-door hardware before replacing or exchanging anything.

Many old-building owners also opted for jamb bolts on their entry doors, especially store owners who wanted extra security. Commercial jamb bolts were usually surface mounted and worked with a pull chain for the upper bolt and a foot-operated spring action on the lower bolt. Residential doors normally had the jamb bolt hidden inside the door stile but also featured a fancy plate mortised flush with the door's surface. The bolt was thrown with a thumb tab that was low enough for easy access. Some homeowners also used horizontal chain bolts for supplemental security, and the late nineteenth century also saw a brisk business in a wide assortment of weird and generally ineffective burglar alarm devices.

Of course, most visitors were of the friendly sort, and as American homes grew larger and larger, folks needed a way to know that someone was at the front door. The traditional doorknocker had slid out of favor by the end of the Civil War due to its clumsy mechanics and primitive noise. In its place the doorbell evolved and became a standard feature for front doors all across the country.

The first doorbells were just that: little brass bells that were attached to springs that made them ring when a wire was pulled. The bells would be mounted on an interior wall, and the wire had to run a circuitous route across and down the wall and then out to the bell pull

Below: American doorknobs can be found in innumerable shapes, materials and designs. These examples include bronze, painted porcelain, pressed and faceted glass, Bennington pottery, cast iron, enamel work and Monel metal. The styles range from Antebellum to Neo-Grec, to Arts and Crafts and even Institutional.

Opposite Left: In the early 1870s you could special order bronze door trim inlaid with colored enamel from the P.F. Corbin Company. Note the eclectic shape of this front door plate and the keyway that has a horizontal opening.

Opposite Top: In the mid-nineteenth century, glass doorknobs could be found in numerous sizes and styles. This is the Dewdrop pattern offered by the Nashua Lock Company in the late 1860s. Solarization caused the nice purple color.

Opposite Bottom: This lock set looks like it may have came from a modern house, but it actually dates back to the 1840s, proving that much of what we think is new is actually very old.

mounted next to the entry door. The local bell hanger had a variety of little moveable guides and pulleys to make his job easier, but by the 1870s, self-contained, door-mounted mechanical bells had taken over the market. These doorbells came in several sizes and had cast-iron bodies and often had bronze tops that were highly decorated. They had spring-action hammers inside, which on some models were tripped with a crank handle and cam gear, and on other models a series of levers. These bells gave out mighty gongs that could be heard throughout those big houses that were being built all across America.

A third type of door-mounted bell used clockwork gears and a thumb turn and generated the distinctive "brrrrring" that has become a hallmark of antique houses. These bells had fancy cases, but they were made in the 1890s and later, when casting quality had declined considerably. Meanwhile, domestic electricity was available as early as the 1870s, so electric doorbells, activated by a little button set next to the door, steadily took over as the ringer of choice.

During the decades of fancy doorbells it was also the habit of the postman to take the mail right to the front door. This meant that many entry doors were fitted with a mail slot, and usually it matched the fancy entrance hardware. Many antique mail slots are too small for today's mail, so if you want to install an old one, look for the "newspapers" model, which is jumbo size and will accommodate just about anything your postman can deliver.

Among the most popular nineteenth-century mail-order items were pattern books filled with house plans. Families all across America were building on their successes and constructing the houses of their dreams. This created an enormous market for fine and fancy hardware, and we continue to enjoy those little architectural gems today.

Below: Fancy bronze "letters" slot dating from the 1870s and featuring fine Neo-Grec decoration.

Right: A pretty, painted porcelain doorknob and keyhole cover can dress up even the plainest-Jane door.

A Survey of Vintage
Lighting

Antique lighting fixtures are among the most abundant resources in any architectural salvage shop. That said, finding the exact chandelier or pan light you're looking for can be a highly frustrating experience. If you find a design you like in the style you envision, the fixture won't be the right size and scale for your room, or vice versa. With persistence, however, you will find a lighting fixture (or even a set of them) that meets your needs.

You should be aware that the older and more rare the fixture, the more expensive it is likely to be. This is especially true for fixtures that in recent years have become collectible purely as antiques: the subtly decorated gaslight fixtures of the mid-nineteenth century, and Arts and Crafts lamps and fixtures signed by iconic makers such as Van Erp, Tiffany or Stickley. Luckily, many styles of light fixtures from the twentieth century are still abundant, including designs for every style of home built in the last hundred years.

Colonial Lighting

All early American lighting was made by hand. Most of it was fairly crude looking: wire-arm chandeliers with painted, turned-wood centers and sheet metal or punched-tin lanterns were far more common than brass-armed chandeliers or crystal candelabra. These were rare

Left: Gothic brass lanterns from the late nineteenth century are wonderful accents in a formal hall or dining room.

Below: A crystal chandelier is casually laid on a table as an elegant, forgotten accent.

treasures in the late eighteenth and nineteenth centuries, imported from Europe and appearing only in the finest homes. Sconces—often as rudimentary as a single candle backed by a square or rounded sheet of polished tin—were much more common. Quaint though it seems today, mirrored sconces with real glass were considered the height of luxury when they first arrived in America around 1730.

Should you find a genuinely old fixture that appears to be colonial, it's likely that your discovery is a reproduction. Colonial-type fixtures, both crude and fancy, have been reproduced for at least 125 years. That doesn't mean your vintage wire-arm chandelier or betty lamp, an early oil lamp, isn't a great find: many colonial-style reproductions are now old enough to be considered antiques on their own merits. The most authentic pieces would have hung from hooks on the ceiling or wall, but many truly old pieces were wired for the adaptation to electricity.

The best vintage pieces look handmade. The wire arms should be slightly less than uniform; the crimps in the tin should have subtle variations that show that an individual, not a machine, made the piece. A brass fixture (usually a dead giveaway that the piece is Colonial Revival) should have a nice patina. If the piece originally had mock wax candles and some are missing, you can get replacements (complete with simulated candle drips) from a number of companies.

Gaslight

Although gaslight lasted only a few decades in the late nineteenth century, there are plenty of true antique Victorian fixtures out there. Having said that, however, many of the finest fixtures sporting four or more arms cost $25,000 and up. These lovely fixtures are decorated with curling Rococo embellishments on the arms and incising on the pole mounts, and often retain the original open-glass shades. Combination

Top Left: An ordinary brass trivet is given a new life when used as a wall sconce in a hallway.

Middle Left: An Arts and Crafts wrought-iron chandelier was found for this New York apartment building lobby to help bring back its original grandeur.

Bottom Left: A rare bronze Tiffany wall sconce in the form of a peacock lights a Turkish room.

Above: An Art Deco chandelier is the perfect accent for the homeowners' collection of 1930s and '40s memorabilia, which includes Bakelite radios.

Left: A finial from a Victorian wrought-iron fence was recycled as an attractive table lamp.

Below: A kitchen sink area is enlivened by lighting from a trio of vintage hanging lights dressed with decorative shades.

Top Right: An unusual amber-colored original glass shade makes this wrought-iron Arts and Crafts overhead fixture the focal point in an entrance foyer.

Middle Right: An ornate brass chandelier in a Victorian study has decorative griffins and leaf motifs. It was originally a gas fixture but was eventually converted to electricity.

Bottom Right: A flashy crystal-and-wrought-iron chandelier, ca. 1940, was found at a flea market and adds an elegant note to this San Francisco dining room.

gas-electric fixtures—with the gas-jetted bowl facing up and the electric-mounted shade facing down—can be more affordable. These fixtures are some of the most delightful designs of the era, and look appropriate in a wide range of turn-of-the-twentieth-century homes.

Even more attractive from a collector's standpoint are sconces (also called bracket lamps) that are made of cast iron or brass, often in whimsical designs like a hand holding a torch. To verify that they're original, look for an embossed manufacturer's signature; some are also stamped with dates or numbers. Victorian fixtures are worth collecting, even if one or more of the glass shades is missing. If you're patient, you can find globed or fluted antique replacements in etched, iridescent, opalescent, tinted or clear glass. Shades for gas fixtures are always open at the top; complementary shades for the electric element on a combination fixture can be closed, and can point downward.

Twentieth-Century Lighting

By far the greatest numbers of fixtures available to the salvage browser are electric lights from the early twentieth century onward. It's still relatively easy to find many styles designed and manufactured for American homes of the teens, twenties, and beyond, from bare-bulb "shower" fixtures to crystal pan fixtures (a pan fixture is mounted flush to the ceiling) in the shape of an inverted pyramid. Hammered copper and mica or slag glass Arts and Crafts fixtures can be quite affordable if they are unsigned. Also widely available are many timeless designs characteristic of the Colonial and Neoclassical Revival styles. Some of the most versatile styles are large, suspended chandeliers with a single translucent or opaque bowl that bounces light off the ceiling for a pleasing, ambient glow.

In order to keep up with demand, an increasing number of dealers are harvesting light fixtures from early-twentieth-century hotels, apartment buildings, and even warehouses and factories. Some of the most common and versatile industrial fixtures available are prismatics. Composed of an inverted shade of clear ribbed glass encased in a spare metal cage, these pendant lights are especially attractive for task lighting (in the kitchen, for example). Also prized for the same reason are schoolhouse-style globe fixtures that hang from a straight pole of almost any length.

Fanciful sconces and chandeliers from the Jazz Age often feature floating slipper shapes of sculpted glass in flamboyant reds, pinks and greens. The style is often reminiscent of women's beaded, slightly swaying clothing of the era. On a more utilitarian note, look for the small porcelain sconces and wall lamps that originally graced baths and kitchens of the 1920s and '30s.

The Machine Age of the 1930s and '40s produced some of the most inventive lighting designs in America. The metal fixtures lean toward sculptural polished chrome, with or without fins, while the opaque or milky-white shades might be in the shape of a spinning top or an inverted ziggurat. Enhancements included banding, either as part of the glass shade itself or as applied ribs of chrome. Some fixtures were also painted with bands of yellow and green paint set off with thin black lines.

Lighting from the 1950s, '60s and '70s is even more widely available, and at every price range. Look for designs that are the purest essence of the era: space-age chrome fixtures from the fifties; sculptural, vase-like ceramic lamps of the sixties; and in the way-out seventies, choose from shades made of plastics, mesh weaves, folded wood veneers, and luminous hand-blown glass. The sky's the limit.

Opposite Top: This Arts and Crafts brass wall sconce is embellished with a period opalescent hobnail shade.

Opposite Bottom: A wall sconce in the shape of a hand was considered the epitome of good taste in a Victorian home, as Queen Victoria herself thought her hands were exceptionally beautiful.

Left: This Arts and Crafts–style wall sconce was actually created from old parts, including an old doorplate.

Below: A whimsical Victorian wall sconce in the form of a dog's head lights a Victorian parlor. Dogs and animals were popular motifs in the late nineteenth century.

The Magic of Mantels

For many lovers of old houses, a room is just a plain box with windows and a door unless it has a fireplace. A fireplace and its mantel are the focal point that transforms a mundane chamber into the centerpiece of a home, something that invites us in and allows us to relax at a cozy hearth. A room's furnishings and decorations are always based around the presence of the mantel, and thus it plays a crucial role in historic design.

Now, to be precise, a *mantel* is the horizontal surface located directly over the fireplace opening upon which we place treasured objects. The fancy wood or stone columns and embellishments that visually and physically support it are referred to as the *surround*. Any architectural structure resting directly on top of the mantel is an *overmantel*. The *hearth* is a stone or tile area directly in front of the fireplace that protects the wooden floor from stray embers.

Mantels appear in varying degrees of ornamentation, and typically parallel the quality of the remainder of a building's architectural trim. As a rule, the fancier the building, the fancier the mantel. However, one is occasionally surprised by a modest home where someone paid for a fancy parlor mantel replete with all the ornamental bells and whistles. The reverse is also true: it's not uncommon to find an upscale structure where either finances or some vestige of Puritanism caused the builders

An Arts and Crafts oak mantel, ca. 1900, is highlighted with period pottery.

to restrain themselves and install something seemingly down-market for the caliber of the house.

For a historically accurate installation, your attitude toward building a mantel should be, "How would it have been done when the house was built?" You should always strive to find a new surround that looks as if it had been there, not as if it were simply found at a tag sale and bolted to the wall because it seemed to fit. Try to avoid upgrading the mantel to a point where it is incongruous with the house. For example, don't put a high-style Renaissance Revival burled walnut surround flanked with caryatids in a humble cottage.

Of course, if you're creating a fantasy, or just not that concerned with historic authenticity, ignore all of this advice and please yourself.

The *firebox* is the small masonry chamber where wood or coal combust—the truly functional part of a fireplace. For those with an existing firebox, making a salvage mantel conform to the predetermined dimensions proves to be the greatest challenge. A new mantel may be adapted in several ways, beginning with a buffer zone of nonflammable material, usually tile, although brick, slate and marble may be used. You may also have to create a filler area that was not quite the originally intended size, but this is the easiest method.

Sometimes wood mantels may be altered slightly by removing or trimming down the inner moldings that cover the rough edge of the tiles. For the adventuresome, you can always take apart the surround and modify the framing elements, much the same as an antique double bed is converted to a king or queen.

When selecting an antique mantel, be downright cynical as you examine a prospective piece. Look for missing parts, as moldings get knocked off easily, especially around the plinths and baseboards or wherever the surround was connected to the wall. Replicating any of

Right: Spindled shelves accent this late-nineteenth-century cherry mantel and are used to display Victorian knickknacks.

Below: A rustic country mantel was fashioned from an ancient wooden beam and hand-laid stones.

Opposite: A handsome Federal-style oak mantel is accented with a tiled surround and becomes the focal point of the room.

Left: A beautiful hand-carved marble mantel, ca. 1860, features foliate designs that were popular during this era.

Middle Left: Pensive, whimsical gnomes support a mahogany mantel, ca. 1930.

Middle Right: The world is kept safely in the arms of this storybook-style mantel, ca. 1925.

Right: A beautifully carved maiden supports the sides of this marble Victorian mantel.

those missing bits can be expensive, as a woodworker will have to "tool up" for it; making six inches of molding is just as expensive as making twenty feet.

Many mantels depart the salvage yard slathered in countless layers of paint, and while the thought of stripping them is daunting, you will always be amazed at the amount of detail that emerges when they are taken down to bare wood, even if it is only to paint them once again. This being said, take extra care to ensure that you don't strip an original faux finish off of your old mantel.

The most common form of decorative or faux painting on surrounds occurred in the mid-nineteenth century: slate was often marbleized with paint to emulate fancy species of stone. If you are fortunate enough to obtain a piece with this treatment, do your best to preserve it, even if you have to in-paint anything that's missing. You will also come across pine or other paint-grade wood surrounds that were grain-painted to look like oak or mahogany; there are usually telltale chips in the finish that go beneath the paint treatment, revealing the primer.

Beware the missing overmantel. From the 1880s through 1910, in the Eastlake and Colonial Revival styles, overmantels were frequently part of the entire structure, incorporating étagères and mirrors, which were usually beveled. The Arts and Crafts movement witnessed the decline in the use of integral overmantels. These overmantels were frequently removed during the twentieth century as they were considered unfashionable. Take extra care to look on the horizontal surface of the mantel itself for the dowel holes that were plugged when the overmantel was removed.

Below: An elegant marble mantel is highlighted against black marble floors in this remodeled Victorian home.

Right: An elaborate mantel from a New York mansion was made the focal point of this glamorous living room.

American mantels from the Federal Period through the middle of the nineteenth century were basically of neoclassical design, composed of columns and/or pilasters supporting an entablature (a horizontal member). Stylistic subtleties were worked in, such as slight Gothic or Adam influences, but until the 1850s, this form was the standard. Of course, the interpretation could range from simplistic dimensionally cut lumber all the way up to reeded or fluted columns with fanciful capitals and applied moldings on the entablature. As a rule, these mantels were painted and rarely clear-finished, or they were marble.

In the 1850s, mantel fashion changed dramatically. The Rococo Revival surround of choice was two flat slabs of stone framing a rounded opening. The seam was concealed with a carved pediment, and this supported a serpentine, molded mantel. The prototypical piece was composed of white Vermont marble, with some incised line-work. From this baseline, things got very fancy—anything that could be carved from stone was added to imply the owner's prosperity, with the finest pieces being carved from exotic stones with unusual colors. For those of more modest means, there were slate and cast-iron mantels in the same form as the more expensive marble.

After a decade or so, marble became less popular (but didn't disappear) with the rise of Eastlake and the revival of medievalism; mantels were now usually wood with tile surrounds to buffer them from the flames. Low-style Eastlake mantels were little more than four paint-grade planks with some cursory railroad-track molding (parallel beaded grooves) decorating their surface, while the high-style pieces incorporated massive integral superstructures replete with many beveled mirrors and étagère shelving. The latter may also have had polychrome, gilt line-work, or, in the finer homes, inlaid varieties of wood.

As there were so many stylistic changes from 1875 to 1900—including Anglo-Japanese, Persian and Colonial Revival—mantels often reflected these nuances, sometimes purely, sometimes gleefully blended. Once again, the more architecturally true to a style a house was, so went the mantel, at least until the 1890s. At this point, the forces of Craftsman, Colonial Revival and late Eastlake would often battle it out within the same home, and it was quite common to see Colonial Revival structures with Mission mantels and Shingle/Craftsman houses sporting Colonial Revival surrounds.

The American Arts and Crafts movement heralded a rejection of Victorian ornamentation, and the more high style the interior, the less it resembled its nineteenth-century forebears. Tiles began to expand outward, negating the need for the usual surround, and copper hoods were also favorites. Defining a lower-style mantel is somewhat confusing, as the Mission style was so restrained that even a more prestigious home could have what we consider a plain mantel. Also popular was the use of face-brick, either red or yellow, laid in a broad, Romanesque arch.

After the turn of the twentieth century, mantels again assumed traditional proportions, especially in the Romantic Revivals of the 1920s. Concurrently, Modernism, with its refutation of ornamentation, banished the surround and permitted the vestigial mantel of a mere suggestion of a horizontal design element that might not even protrude from the wall. Even with this eradication of the surround, the fireplace was still the visual center of any given room.

Mirrored blue glass from a 1930s movie palace was salvaged to make this unusual, stylish mantel.

Left: An English oak mantel, ca. 1910, makes a welcoming statement in this Southern cottage furnished with salvaged treasures.

Right: Note the built-in bookshelves in the mantel. An old iron fence is cleverly recycled as a firescreen.

The Secrets of
Sinks

A weathered, slate sink in a New York kitchen is operated by both conventional hand knobs as well as brass foot pedals used in hospital operating rooms.

During the past two hundred years, American sinks have evolved from dry to wet to wonderful. At first they were little more than a carved-out stone or a large bucket, but as the kitchen steadily expanded, innovative homeowners demanded better-looking and more functional fixtures. Sinks for personal use soon became a standard item in bed chambers, and by the mid-nineteenth century, they were well on their way to having a room of their own: the bath. It wasn't long before these handy plumbing pieces also spread to basements, laundry rooms, garden rooms, summer kitchens, greenhouses and patios. Pairs, doubles, colors and combinations made sinks more useful and attractive, and the great designs at the turn of the twentieth century presented them as works of art.

Over time, most plumbing functions have remained constant, but the shapes, styles and decorations have evolved and cycled, depending on trends and technology. The current rage is retro, so whether it is eighteenth-, nineteenth- or twentieth-century design you desire, vintage is in!

Due to strong demand and limited quantities, especially in the past several decades, a large reproduction market has arisen in the United States. And because many pieces found in the vintage market are not in good condition, refinishing businesses are also flourishing. But nothing can take the place of the real thing—the glow of an old finish and the great design found only in a period piece. It may take some time to locate the sink of your dreams, but the hunt will be an adventure and the results well worth the trip.

In preparation for buying a vintage sink it is important to decide what type of sink best fits your interior and your lifestyle. Be sure of your plans and measurements, and recognize that no vintage sink will be perfect—period pieces have had a long life and often have the scars to prove it! Choose quality in style, function and condition. And most important, find a plumber who appreciates antiques and looks at vintage plumbing as a special project both he and the homeowner can enjoy.

Bathroom Sinks

Sinks for the bathroom were made in two basic styles: freestanding pedestals and wall-mounted sinks, with or without legs. Both styles were available in several materials.

Earthenware sinks are formed from porous clay, coated with white slip, and then kiln fired. A final finish of thick, clear glaze and another firing gives earthenware its eggshell-white color. Over time, due to the expansion and contraction of the clay, the glaze will craze and develop a wonderful surface. Most wall-mounted earthenware sinks had two front legs made of either nickel-plated brass or matching earthenware. Such sinks often had a backsplash as well. Some corner sinks had a single "peg" leg, and earthenware pedestal sinks always had an earthenware pedestal. Earthenware is considered the most desirable by collectors of antique plumbing and is perfect for traditional and country interiors.

Porcelain used for sinks (and toilets) is a white clay with a glazed finish. It is much denser and whiter than earthenware and can be formed into more delicate shapes. Porcelain was used for toilets in the

Above: This "bar sink" is typical of sinks found in soda fountains, restaurants and bars ca. 1900. It is made of nickel-plated copper wrapped around a wood frame. The original towel bar, milkglass front skirt and single cold water faucet over a deep sink bowl suggest this may have come from an ice cream parlor. Today, interesting sinks such as this are often installed in bars, kitchens, pantries and garden rooms.

Middle Left: The "Mae West" pedestal sink, ca. 1920s, nicknamed for the voluptuous "waist and hips" in the pedestal, illustrates how manufacturers began casting iron in decorative and unusual styles. The Mae West and Martini sinks use the same sink top placed on different bases, creating two totally different "flavors" of design.

Middle Right: This earthenware pedestal sink illustrates how the same material can work with a variety of decorating styles. Changes in shape and styling created this charming, though simpler, sink.

Lower Left: A beautiful earthenware pedestal sink, ca. 1900. A simple molded edge combined with a subtle swell on the front apron and placed on a paneled pedestal becomes a stunning focal point for a turn-of-the-century bath restoration or re-creation.

Lower Right: A companion in style, quality, and date to the "Mae West" was the "Martini" sink. More deco in style, this cast-iron sink determines the design of the rest of the room.

nineteenth century and became more popular for sinks around 1900. You can find both pedestal and wall-mounted porcelain sinks, most often in white but also in a wide assortment of colors. Porcelain works well in more formal, tailored interiors, or twentieth-century restorations, but some porcelain sinks are so elegant in their simplicity of line that they are at home in modern interiors as well.

Marble is a soft, somewhat porous stone that will absorb materials left on the surface. Quite often you will see marble sink tops with dark stains, usually caused by the fats used in old soap. There are processes that may clean some of these stains, but generally they are there to stay. Great old marble sinks are rich and mellow, so focus on the history and character and forget about the blemishes.

Marble was very popular for sinks from the mid-1880s through the early 1900s. The standard style was a white marble deck and backsplash with a porcelain undermount bowl. Early on, marble sinks were placed in corners or niches in bedrooms, or sometimes in pass-throughs between two bedrooms, where they could be shared. They appeared in halls, in closets, on porches and wherever resourceful homeowners deemed necessary. Marble was easy to cut and shape, making unusual applications practical.

Gradually, designated rooms for bathing developed and more elaborate marble sinks were designed. Some had massive backsplashes, elaborate nickel-plated brackets and decorated porcelain sink bowls. Many had fancy faucetry, including figural chain-stays that held your rings while you washed your hands. Some of the best-quality sinks sat on fancy legs that not only held up the sink but also supported a marble apron that added a new dimension to sink design. Colored marbles and onyx also became trendy during this time.

Enameled iron was the most common material used in sinks in the nineteenth and twentieth centuries. It was easy to manufacture, affordable and perfect for the booming housing market. Enameled bathtubs were catching on fast, so making bath, kitchen and even laundry sinks was a natural addition to a plumbing manufacturer's line. Every manufacturer and contracting company had its own catalogs of fixtures and accessories that were often cast with the company name, whether it was actually the manufacturer or not.

Kitchen Sinks

Sinks for the kitchen came in a larger variety of materials than did bath sinks. Enameled iron was used most often, but kitchen sinks were also made from slate, soapstone, copper, German silver and Monel metal. Many of the earliest sinks were wood boxes; those were replaced by cast-iron troughs placed in wood cabinets, now quite desirable in country decorating.

Slate is a natural, common stone that was cut into one-inch slabs, like wood boards, mortised and screwed together, and then sealed at the seams. Slate has a charcoal color in its natural state and can be used without sealing the surface. However, when seasoned with mineral oil, slate changes to a soft black color that can be a dynamic focal point for a traditional or modern kitchen.

Soapstone is also a natural stone that is cut and assembled in the same manner as slate. It has a naturally blue-gray mottled texture with a soft, soapy-feeling surface, thus its name. It doesn't have to be sealed and wears well. The look is traditional, warm and inviting. Both slate and soapstone sinks may show cracks or leak around the joints. Modern epoxies, however, make sealing joints or repairing leaks easy.

Upper Left: If one sink wasn't adequate, doubles fit the need for individuality and grand design statements. Two bowls on a single pedestal was, and remains, rare. This porcelain sink dates from the 1930s and measures a full forty-eight inches wide. Notice how the deco-inspired triple-stepped motif in the skirt repeats around the foot of the pedestal.

Upper Middle: This sink bowl is a fine hand-painted example of fourth-quarter nineteenth-century decorated porcelain. It is shown as would be installed—under a marble sink top. Notice that there is only one faucet—cold— a very common occurance in early sink installations. Hot water and devices to heat the water were developing simultaneously with indoor plumbing concepts.

Upper Right: This compact deco design from the 1930s followed the popular style of its day. Although the sink measures only forty-four inches, the designers packed a lot of function into a small space by mounting the faucets on the top of the backsplash, which also covered the water lines. Cast-iron sinks with deep skirts like this one are the most sought-after by educated consumers.

Lower Left: JL Mott earthenware wall-mounted bath sink on nickel-plated legs, ca. 1897. The wall brackets are designed to hold the sink away from the wall, making the sink appear to "float" near the wall. This sink is extraordinary considering the date—a perfect example of nineteenth-century technology adapted to twenty-first-century design.

Lower Middle: Cast-iron, wall-mounted corner sink with backsplash, ca. 1910–20, includes the original hardware. This delightful 24-x-22-inch wall sink was affordable, offered practical applications for small spaces and still had style.

Lower Right: The cabinet sink was both popular and practical in the fourth quarter of the nineteenth century. This example shows a marble top with a fancy backsplash on a walnut cabinet. These sinks were placed in bedrooms, halls, and large closets, and then into rooms transformed into bathrooms as the concept of a separate bathing room caught on and advancing technology provided.

Copper in sinks is as tricky as copper in cookware. Many homeowners fantasize about an old copper sink in the kitchen but fail to consider the maintenance. Copper tarnishes quickly and dents easily; however, small copper sinks were used in the pantry, where they received less abuse. Old copper sinks are available, but many were originally nickel-plated and have been stripped. If you do find an old copper sink, beware that copper oxidizes quickly, so if you don't have a scullery maid to do the polishing, you are in for a good bit of extra work.

German silver is actually nickel-plated copper and was popular for pantry and kitchen sinks in the early 1900s. This was the metal of choice in finer homes before stainless steel became the standard for similar applications. Nickel plated onto copper creates a warm silver color, but like any plated materials, the nickel wears through, leaving some copper showing. Today, that mellow vintage look is very desirable and adds a comfy, lived-here-forever look. Old German silver sinks are quite difficult to find, although new ones are being reproduced by one of the original manufacturers.

Monel metal is an alloy of brass and nickel and is sometimes called *white brass*. It looks very much like German silver. It is warmer in color than stainless steel but cooler than German silver. Like stainless steel, it does not wear through. Monel metal was popular in the early twentieth century and can be found in both commercial and residential kitchen applications. Monel metal sinks are also hard to find, but like all high-quality antiques, the result justifies the time, effort and expense.

Plumbers & Plumbing

My plumber says there is nothing that can't be done if you want to do it. Most plumbers are famous for saying, "It can't be done" which really means "I don't want to do it." Finding a plumber who likes to work with old fixtures is not easy, but if you persevere you can find someone to do a proper job. The basic process and skills for hooking up water and setting sinks have not changed for a hundred years, so you're not asking someone to reinvent the wheel. Find the restoration contractors in your area and talk with them. Then interview tradesmen and be very specific about what you want. It is always best to have the old fixtures at hand so you and the plumber can see exactly how the rough-in work will be done.

Notes on Materials

- Porcelain and earthenware cannot be reglazed and I do not recommend refinishing.

- Enameled iron can be refinished but the results and longevity are poor.

- Slate and soapstone may crack but can be successfully sealed. They wear well.

- Marble is hard to clean and easy to break if mishandled. Once installed it will wear well. Be careful when moving or storing marble as it breaks easily, especially if laid flat.

- German silver oxidizes over time, so clean with a soft cloth and don't use abrasive cleaners.

Left Top: This ca. 1920s sink is made from Monel metal, also known as white brass. Used in the early twentieth century in kitchens and commercial applications, it was rugged yet beautiful. It was originally expensive, and this makes the number of available vintage Monel sinks few.

Left Bottom: This ca. 1910–20s German silver double sink with drain boards, though designed for a kitchen, ended up being a dynamic bath sink surrounded by mirrors, proving that a great sink and a little imagination can do wonders for your vintage plumbing project.

Above: A beautiful example of a copper pantry sink mounted under a chestnut countertop. These date from the turn of the twentieth century, when homes often had a separate pantry room, with its own sink, adjoining the kitchen. Pantry sinks are extremely desirable today for kitchen, bar, garden and outdoor kitchen applications.

Stairs & Staircases
Savoir-Faire

If you've ever admired a beautifully crafted staircase in a house built a century or more ago and wished you could add one to your home, you can. Staircases and many of the parts that combine to make them are among the most striking and versatile types of architectural salvage available today. It's possible to find completely intact staircases, as well as individual components that can be adapted in a new stair installation, or unique applications of your own design. The only limitation is your imagination and the skill of your builder or carpenter.

Don't think that you are limited only to wood when shopping for staircase parts. Many of the most unique and stunning pieces of architectural salvage come from buildings such as old hotels and apartment houses and can incorporate or be made from such materials as wrought iron, bronze or even aluminum. Stair components that can usually be adapted to new uses include newel posts, banisters, handrails, slats and spindles, treads and risers, and the paneling and wainscots that formerly trimmed or partially enclosed the stairway.

Newels

Newels are the starting point for any staircase. They are also typically the finishing point for a handrail or banister. The newel can be a separate element, like a hand-height post with a finished top, or an

A weathered wrought-iron newel post is combined with turned wooden spindles for a unique vintage look.

integrated extension of the handrail. Because newel posts are usually the most prominent and decorative feature of any staircase, they're in great demand by those who want to restore a set of stairs or build a new one. The simplest shapes are square or cylindrical, with minimal shaping or decoration. Shaped newels are usually formed by turning them on a mechanical lathe, which results in the elaborate rounded and beaded shapes found in staircases in Victorian or early-twentieth-century homes. While many newels in the Arts and Crafts style of the early 1900s are square, they're often decorated on all four sides with trim pieces to give them a greater sense of depth.

Newels can be finished with a simple rectangular or tapered handgrip, but they are often topped with finials of various shapes, such as carved balls or pineapples. In the case of Victorian staircases, the most elaborate type of decoration is a three-dimensional metal figure, with or without light fixture. (The female figures in flowing toga-style robes are called Spelter Maidens.) Usually these pieces get separated from the newel, but if you are fortunate enough to find one that's intact, you've made a rare discovery indeed.

If you're planning on adapting a newel post to a new or existing staircase, you may have to modify the newel by either adding or reducing its height—preferably with material that accentuates its design. Newel posts should be built to comfortable hand height (about four feet). This allows the newel to serve as a physical and visual anchor for the staircase as well as a convenient place to put your hand as you ascend the stairs.

Banisters and Handrails

Most flights of stairs have both a handrail and vertical supports, commonly square or tapered spindles, that link the handrail to the stair

Salvaged oak newel posts and spindles were found for this country home staircase in California.

treads. Put together, this combination is called a banister. Handrails that have lost their spindles are often available; the nicest are made of high-quality hardwoods that are shaped on the top and molded on the sides to make them easier to grip. If you're looking for a handrail to finish an existing stair or incorporate into a new design, try to find a salvaged piece that is longer than the run you need. Otherwise you'll have to splice new wood into the salvaged handrail and stain the entire railing in such a way that the seam doesn't show. In either case, you'll need an experienced carpenter to adapt the old piece into your project.

Banisters complete with the original slats, spindles or turned balusters are another excellent find. They can be more difficult to adapt into new settings because they were built (sometimes in place) to fill a space with specific angles and a given room height. Again, you'll need a skilled carpenter to make nips and tucks to get your find to fit into the setting you envision. (It helps if you find the staircase or banister *before* you decide on ceiling heights and room plans.)

Slats, Spindles and Balusters

Banisters and handrails are usually supported by square, rounded or tapered supports called spindles, or flat supports called slats. The supports on more elaborate staircases (especially those made of stone or wood that have been formed on a mechanical lathe) are called balusters. The simplest spindles and slats are often spaced closely together. In more complex constructions, the spindles may be grouped in twos and threes to rest on an individual stair tread.

If you're looking for one or two spindles of a common design to replace missing pieces in an existing period stair, you should be able to find these by looking on the Internet (an alternative is to have a matching replacement newly milled). On the other hand, it's possible

A metal post and finial from France make an elegant statement for this San Francisco staircase. The crusty patina was carefully preserved as part of the newel post's charm.

to stumble upon a full set of uniquely shaped spindles or slats with decorative cutouts that inspire a wholly new creation.

Since spindles are three-dimensional, they can vary extraordinarily, even in a single staircase. (Turned spindles from fancy Neoclassical Revival staircases, for example, might afford three or four slightly different patterns in a single flight.) Spindles can also be spaced to create a repeating pattern (for instance, a grouping of two spindles followed by a grouping of three, followed by two) or combined with crossbars or insets. Only your imagination limits the choices.

Slats, especially, lend themselves to cutout designs. The cutouts can be geometric shapes like a circle or zigzag, or of a natural element like an acorn or gingko leaf. The cutout patterns were made by tracing the pattern onto one slat or two adjoining slats and then cutting the pattern out with a jigsaw.

Treads and Risers

The tread is the working part of the stair—the part we walk on. Risers, on the other hand, are the vertical boards that link one tread to the next. You can adapt old stair steps into new projects (e.g., a couple of steps down to a sunken living room, a built-in step ladder to a high bookcase) or re-use them in a new staircase. While the treads are usually the most worn-out part of any stair, boards in sound condition may be made of old-growth wood that's developed a patina as well as interesting undulations from decades of footsteps. Just be sure the old steps are in good enough shape to support the weight of a full-grown adult carrying a heavy object. If the wood is soft (like old pine boards), you can reinforce them with new boards underneath.

Paneling and Wainscots

Wall panels and wainscots are built-up decorative finishes on the lower portion of a wall. The wall paneling that trims out an old staircase is often some of the finest salvage material found in a house or building. Designs include raised-panel motifs in beautifully mellowed wood and wainscots finished with embossed leather or a vintage material like Lincrusta or Anaglypta. The catch is that these panels have usually been adapted to follow the diagonal path of the stair as it moves from one floor to another. This means that the center panels in a raised-panel design might be parallelograms rather than rectangles. The panels may also be different dimensions, sized to the demands of the original installation. If you're lucky enough to have found an exceptional section of wood paneling or wainscoting that you'd like to incorporate in your home, consider creating a project that suits its dimensions. Another alternative is to adapt a smaller portion of the paneling to your needs.

The crusty patina of a weathered iron newel post was carefully preserved as part of its charm and attraction.

Left: Wrought-iron exterior fencing and posts were recycled as an interior staircase in a San Francisco home.

Right: An ornate, burled-walnut Renaissance Revival newel post is the center of attraction for this New York townhouse staircase.

Stained Glass
Savvy

Stained glass sets the tone of a room. It can add color and interest, changing the quality of the light and the hue of the furnishings, giving another dimension to the room's design. Stained glass can perform many functions, from hiding an unattractive outdoor feature to providing privacy inside, and can be used just about anywhere in the home. Odd pieces of glass can even be hung as works of art.

Many people shy away from antique pieces, being concerned about the cost of restoration or whether the glass will fit an existing opening. But don't worry; you don't need to be in awe of stained glass. If a window does not fit exactly (and most don't) you can always add or subtract a piece of glass to make it fit the space. And don't turn away from curving or buckling glass, as the window may still be strong enough for many more years of enjoyment. Try the finger-drumming test: if you drum on the glass with your fingers and don't hear a rattle, then the lead is still tight and the window secure. If the panes do rattle, then the putty has dried to the point that sections of glass are loose in their lead cames (channels) and will need to be stabilized.

But even stabilizing loose glass is not complicated. For simple repairs, try taking a little putty, darkening it with lamp black, and pushing it into the areas that are loose using your fingers or a blunt piece of wood. Let the putty dry for a few days, then trim off the excess

A colorful opaque slag-glass window from the early twentieth century blends in perfectly in this cheerful room in Texas filled with salvage and flea market treasures.

with a putty knife and your window will be as good as new. You can also try mixing the putty with linseed oil, a time-honored method of repair, which makes it easier to brush onto the window. Just wipe off the excess with a newspaper and your window will now be stiffer and more airtight. Don't forget that cracked glass is much like the nicks and dents on old furniture—part of the charm and patina. Unless the glass is ready to fall out, a crack is best left alone and can often be made more secure by gluing it with clear epoxy cement. If you have a sagging window that can be easily removed from its sash, leave it on a flat surface for several days and the sag will right itself. But be careful—handling an old piece of glass out of its sash is much like handling a large pancake.

To be honest, good old glass is hard to find, especially when you need several matching windows or want a particular pattern, style or color. While new stained glass does not have the patina and character of the old, it is nonetheless readily available and can be custom fit to a particular space and palette. And new glass does not have the maintenance and repair concerns of older glass.

Often it's a combination of old and new glass that best meets the needs. When I discovered an unusual pressed-glass panel of a stork, I knew I had to find a place for it. But the antique window was only half as large as the sash I had in mind for it, a transom above a door. So I had a custom wooden sash built that incorporated the old window in its center, then accented it with new rondels of amber-colored glass and thick leading around the perimeter to fill in the rest of the frame. It now looks like it has always been there.

What tips do the experts have for maintaining your stained glass? Don't expose the lead to the elements, as it will eventually leak as the putty weakens. Storm sashes protect your windows from damage as well

Below: A nineteenth-century French café sign painted on glass is given a new lease on life when it is hung on a wall in a salvage-savvy home.

Right: An early-twentieth-century paneled window has been reinstalled in a parlor filled with unusual salvage finds.

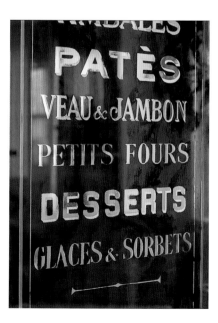

Left: An antique stained glass window from a French cathedral becomes the focal point for this New York kitchen and complements a similar large window in the home's living room.

Right: A bat glides across the night sky in this hand-painted, Aesthetic movement stained glass window. The purple-and-green checkerboard design is new glass added to fill in the window.

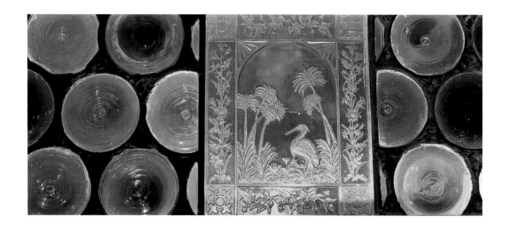

Upper Left: An unusual pressed-glass Victorian panel of a stork was combined with new roundels of amber stained glass for this window transom. Note the leading that was purposefully applied in a heavy fashion to lend age and character to the window.

Lower Left: Whimsical stained glass animals were hand painted on this late-nineteenth-century window found in London's Portobello flea market.

Right: Colorful nineteenth-century stained glass from a church is given new life as a window in a study in Vermont.

as the elements, and can be made nearly invisible. When cleaning, a simple solution of mild kitchen soap followed by a glass-cleaning agent such as Windex works best. Dry with a lint-free towel or newspaper. And if the window is in a bathroom or area where moisture causes the solder lines to become chalky ("foxing"), very fine steel wool will remove the chalkiness and return the solder lines to their original patina. Stops behind glass doors are imperative to prevent breakage from a strong wind or a rambunctious child. And for those living in earthquake country, skylights should be supported on a protective surface, such as a quarter-inch section of Plexiglas, that supports the window and helps prevent it from falling to the floor.

An oversized
mirrored window
from a hotel was
installed in this
New York living
room to become an
instant work of art.

Stained Glass Vocabulary

Here are some of the common terms you can encounter in stained glass:

Stained Glass: Any colored flat glass.

Flashed Glass: Glass of one color that has a thin layer of another color glass on the other side. Often used for ruby red glass.

Leaded Glass: Any glass, clear or colored, that is held together with lead cames.

Rondel: A piece of glass that is spun into a circular shape, either mouth-blown or machine-made.

Solder: Alloy of tin and lead used to bond metals in both leaded and copper-foil glass.

Jewel: A small piece of glass faceted into a geometric shape simulating a real jewel.

Opalescent Glass: Glass that has become opaque by allowing crystallization during its production.

Copper Foil: Thin strips of copper tape used to wrap glass, which are then soldered together.

Crackle Glass: Glass that has been given multiple small fractures and then reheated and fused, the resulting glass resembling alligator skin.

Came: Strips of lead, zinc or sometimes other metals made into channels to hold glass pieces in a pattern.

Left: Not all stained glass needs to be set into a window. This lovely Aesthetic movement stained glass window from England rests between ornate silk curtains on a windowsill.

Right: Reverse-painted glass panels have their designs painted on the back (reverse) but made to show through in the proper direction (much like the silvering on a mirror). Panels from a Roaring Twenties restaurant were installed as colorful privacy windows in a high-style San Francisco bathroom.

Resources

Hardware

Ball and Ball

463 W. Lincoln Hwy.

Exton, PA 19341

Telephone: 610-363-7330

Fax: 610-363-7639

Website: www.ballandball-us.com

E-mail: bill@ballandball-us.com

Antique hardware reproductions: door, window, shutter & furniture hardware, fireplace tools; wrought iron/steel, bronze, brass, copper, cast iron; custom reproductions.

Crown City Hardware

1047 North Allen Ave.

Pasadena, CA 91104

Telephone: 626-794-0234

Fax: 626-794-2064

Website: www.crowncityhardware.com

E-mail: questions@restoration.com

Antique and restoration hardware: glass knobs, bin pulls, hinges, hooks, window/cabinet/bath hardware; iron, brass, glass & crystal; original antique hardware.

Ed Donaldson Hardware Restoration

1488 North Rd.

Carlisle, PA 17013

Telephone: 717-249-3624

Fax: 717-249-5647

Website: www.eddonaldson.com

E-mail: ed@eddonaldson.com

Old and vintage hardware, restored antique hardware, new parts and pieces, Victorian locks.

Eugenia's Antique Hardware

5370 Peachtree Rd.

Chamblee, GA 30341

Telephone: 800-337-1677, 770-458-5966

Fax: 770-458-5966

Website: www.eugeniaantiquehardware.com

E-mail: eugeniashardware@mindspring.com

Door knockers, hinges, doorplates, rosettes, twist bells, furniture and bathroom hardware.

Historic Houseparts

540 South Ave.

Rochester, NY 14620

Telephone: 888-558-2329

Website: www.historichouseparts.com

Vintage and reproductions: hardware, lighting, mantels, bath fixtures, stained glass, doors, windows, radiators, plumbing, cabinetry, shutters.

House of Antique Hardware

3439 NE Sandy Blvd., P.M.B. #106

Portland, OR 97232

Telephone: 888-223-2545, 503-231-4089

Fax: 503-233-1312

Website: www.houseofantiquehardware.com

Door hardware and accessories: rare and ornate hardware; antique styles; historic reproductions.

VictorianHardware.Com

P.O. Box 258, 20 Spahr Rd.

Washington, ME 04574

Telephone: 207-845-2270

Website: www.victorianhardware.com

E-mail: jspahr@pivot.net

Fine Victorian brass, bronze, and cast-iron hardware and related antiques.

WebWilson.com

P.O. Box 506

Portsmouth, RI 02871

Telephone: 800-508-0022

Fax: 401-682-2656

Website: www.webwilson.com

E-mail: hww@webwilson.ccom

Number-one Internet resource for antique hardware, featuring a virtual museum and record-setting online auctions.

Lighting

Architectural Antiquities

Harborside, ME 04642

Telephone: 207-326-4938

Website: www.archantiquities.com

E-mail: sales@archantiquities.com

Hardware, lighting, fireplace items, Victorian plumbing fixtures, stained glass, doors, windows.

Architectural Heritage

2807 Second Ave. S.

Birmingham, AL 35233

Telephone: 205-322-3538

Fax: 205-323-0084

Website: www.architecturalheritage.com

E-mail: Laura@architecturalheritage.com

Lighting, mantels, doors, garden, statuary, decorative items.

Aurora Lampworks

172 N. 11th St.

Brooklyn, NY 11211

Telephone: 718-384-6039

Fax: 718-384-6198

Website: www.auroralampworks.com

E-mail: ask@auroralampworks.com

Restoration, reproduction of historical and custom lighting fixtures.

The Brass Knob

2311 18th St. NW

Washington, DC 20009

Telephone: 202-332-3370

Fax: 202-332-5594

Website: thebrassknob.com

E-mail: bk@thebrassknob.com

Hardware, extensive lighting, mantels, stained glass, decorative items.

City Lights Antique Lighting

2226 Massachusetts Ave.

Cambridge, MA 02140

Telephone: 617-547-1490

Fax: 617-479-2-74

Website: www.citylights.nu

E-mail: lights@citylights.nu

Antique American and European light fixtures, many types and styles.

City Salvage—Architectural Salvage and Antiques

505 1st Ave. NE

Minneapolis, MN 55413-2209

Telephone: 612-627-9107

Website: www.citysalvage.com

E-mail: mail@citysalvage.com

American only. Lighting, mantels, plumbing fixtures, stained glass, millwork, furniture, other architecturals.

Omega Too

2204 San Pablo Ave.

Berkeley, CA 94702

Telephone: 510-843-3636

Fax: 510-843-0666

Website: www.omegatoo.com

Antique and reproduction lighting, bathroom fixtures and accessories, stained glass, Craftsman-style doors, more.

Seattle Building Salvage

330 Westlake Ave. N

Seattle, WA 98103

Telephone 206-381-3453

2114 Hewitt Ave.

Everett, WA 98201

Telephone: 425-303-8500

Fax: 425-783-0529

Website: www.seattlebuildingsalvage.com

Hardware, lighting, plumbing fixtures, stained glass, doors, windows, architectural house parts.

Mantels

Architectural Elements

2202 E. Admiral Blvd.

Tulsa, OK 74110

Telephone: 877-506-7950, 918-382-7950

Website: www.arc-elements.com

E-mail: arc-elements@juno.com

Light fixtures, fireplace mantels, doors, windows, wrought iron, much more; local and regional sources.

Architectural Heritage

2807 Second Ave. S

Birmingham, AL 35233

Telephone: 205-322-3538

Fax: 205-323-0084

Website: www.architecturalheritage.com

E-mail: Laura@architecturalheritage.com

Lighting, mantels, doors, garden, statuary, decorative items.

Architectural Salvage, Inc.

3 Mill St.

Exeter, NH, 03833

Telephone: 603-773-5635

Fax: 603-773-5635

Website: www.oldhousesalvage.com

Extensive hardware, lighting, mantels, bath fixtures, stair parts, doors, windows, flooring, floor registers, iron work, complete doorways and molding.

Materials Unlimited

2 West Michigan Ave.

Ypsilanti, MI 48197

Telephone: 800-299-9462

Fax: 734-482-3636

Website: www.materialsunlimited.com

Restored lighting, mantels, stained and beveled glass windows, doors, furniture.

Olde Good Things (NY) (PA)

124 W. 24th St.

New York, NY, 10011

Telephone: 212-989-8401

Fax: 212-463-8005

400 Gilligan St., Scranton, PA 18508

Telephone: 570-341-7668

Website: www.oldegoodthings.com

eBay store: oldegoodthings

E-mail: mail@oldegoodthings.com

Antique hardware, mantels, plumbing fixtures, stained glass, reclaimed wood flooring, doors, windows, moldings, ironwork, terra-cotta, more.

Portland Architectural Salvage

919 Congress St.

Portland, ME 04101

Telephone: 207-780-0634

Website: www.portlandsalvage.com

E-mail: preserve@portlandsalvage.com

Hardware, lighting, mantels, plumbing, stair parts, stained and leaded glass, doors, windows, columns, shutters, furniture, garden items, more.

Recycling The Past

381 North Main St.

Barnegat, NJ 08005

Telephone: 609-660-9790

Fax: 800-878-3251

Website: www.recyclingthepast.com

E-mail: recycling@comcast.net

Hardware, lighting fixtures, mantels, kitchen & bath, stained glass, doors, columns, windows, garden antiques, wrought iron, newel posts, gingerbread, molding, Victorian pieces, porches, tiles, more.

Tony's Architectural Salvage

123 N. Olive St.

Orange, CA 92866

Telephone: 714-538-1900

Fax: 714-538-1966

Website: www.tonysarchitecturalsalvage.com

E-mail: thesalvageking@msn.com

Hardware, lighting, mantels, plumbing fixtures, staircases, stained and beveled glass, stone and marble statues, gates, fencing, grilles, wood carvings, beams, doors, windows, columns, more.

Sinks

Admac Salvage

111 Saranac St.

Littleton, NH 03561

Telephone: 603-444-1200

Fax: 603-444-1211

Website: www.admacsalvage.com

E-mail: admac@ncia.net

Period hardware, lighting, and plumbing fixtures, mantels, leaded and stained glass, doors, windows, porch parts, claw-foot tubs, slate, marble, brick.

Affordable Antique Bath & More

3888 De Sabla Rd.

Cameron Park, CA 95682

Telephone: 888-303-2284, 530-677-9121

Fax: 530-677-1413

Website: www.bathandmore.com

E-mail: sales@bathandmore.com

Antiques, reproductions; plumbing fixtures, claw-foot tubs, pedestal sinks, faucets, pull-chain toilets, shower rods, other.

LooLoo Design

255 Bristol Ferry Rd.

Portsmouth, RI 02871

Telephone: 800-508-0022

Website: www.looloodesign.com

E-mail: Jill@LooLooDesign.com

Antique plumbing fixtures and bath accessories.

New England Demolition and Salvage
3065 Cranberry Hwy., Unit 6
East Wareham, MA 02538
Telephone: 508-291-7258
Website: www.nedsalvage.com
E-mail: homeneds@aol.com
Sinks, claw foot tubs, doors, windows, radiators, cabinets, hearths, shutters, columns.

Ohmega Salvage General Store
2400 San Pablo Ave.
Berkeley, CA 94702
Telephone: 510-204-0767
Fax: 510-843-7123
Website: www.ohmegasalvage.com
E-mail: ohmegasalvage@earthlink.net
Hardware, lighting, mantels, plumbing fixtures, doors, windows, cabinets, decorative elements.

Santa Fe Wrecking Company
1600 South Santa Fe Ave.
Los Angeles, CA 90021
Telephone: 213-623-3119
Website: www.santafewrecking.com
Hardware, lighting, plumbing fixtures, doors, windows, appliances, more.

Shaver Brothers
eBay auctions
32 Perrine St.
Auburn, NY 13021
Telephone: 800-564-7206
Website: www.shaverbrothers.com
Hardware, lighting, sinks, stained glass windows, doors, windows, porch posts, radiators, claw-foot bathtubs, shutters, hardwood flooring, corbels, fencing, moldings, more. Custom millwork and restoration.

Vintage Plumbing
Website sales only
9645 Sylvia Ave.
Northridge, CA 91324
Telephone: 818-772-1721
Website: www.vintageplumbing.com
E-mail: vintageplumbing@sbcglobal.net
Victorian to Arts & Crafts American bath fixtures: pedestal sinks, unusual toilets and baths, rib-cage showers, unique accessories; repair & replacement of broken or missing parts.

Staircases

Armadillo-South Architectural Salvage, Inc.
4801 Washington Ave.
New Orleans, LA 70125
Telephone: 504-486-1150
Fax: 504-324-6890
Website: www.armadillo-south.com
E-mail: sales@armadillo-south.com
Mantels, plumbing fixtures, stair parts, doors and entryways, windows, millwork, lumber, bricks, marble, fencing and gates, cypress beams, roof tiles, antique slate, more.

Caravati's Inc.
104 East 2nd St.
Richmond, VA 23224
Telephone: 804- 232- 4175
Fax: 804 233 7109
Website: www.recentruins.com
Lighting, mantels, plumbing fixtures, stairway components, stained glass, doors, windows, shutters, columns, flooring, beams, roofing slate, more.

Legacy Building Supply
540 Division St.
Cobourg, Ontario
Telephone: 905-373-0796
Website: www.legacybs.com
Hardware, mantels, bathroom fixtures, plumbing, staircases, stained glass, doors, windows, fireplace items, radiators, bricks, beams and reclaimed lumber, flooring.

North Shore Architectural Antiques
521 7th St.
Two Harbors, MN 55616
Telephone: (218) 834-0018
Website: www.north-shore-architectural-antiques.com
Lighting, mantels, plumbing and fixtures, stairway components, doors, windows, ceiling tin, electrical, tile, stone and pavers, columns, more.

Old House Parts Company
24 Blue Wave Mall
Kennebunk, ME 04043
Telephone: 207-985-1999; Fax: 207-985-1911
Website: www.oldhouseparts.com
E-mail: Parts@OldHouseParts.com
Antique hardware, lighting, mantels, plumbing fixtures, stairway parts, doors, windows, reclaimed wood, garden elements and miscellaneous.

Salvage One
1840 West Hubbard St.
Chicago, IL 60622
Telephone: 312-733-0098; Fax: 312-733-6829
Website: www.salvageone.com
E-mail: staff@salvageone.com
Lighting, mantels and accessories, plumbing fixtures, stairway parts, doors, windows, garden ornaments, lightning rods.

Southern Accents Architectural Antiques

308 2nd Ave. SE

Cullman, AL 35055

Telephone: 205 737 0554

Website: www.antiques-architectural.com

E-mail: info@antiques-architectural.com

Lighting, mantels, bath fixtures, stairway components, beveled and stained glass, doors, antique entryways, ironwork, more.

Steptoe & Wife Architectural Antiques

90 Tycos Drive

Toronto, Ontario, M6B 1V9, Canada

Telephone: 416-780-1707; 800-461-0060

Fax: 416-780-1814

Website: www.steptoewife.com

E-mail: info@steptoewife.com

Staircases, railings, metalwork, tin ceilings, drapery and drapery hardware

White River Architectural Salvage and Antiques

1325 West 30th St.

Indianapolis, IN 46208

Telephone: 800-262-3389

Website: www.whiteriversalvage.com

Lighting, plumbing fixtures, staircase components, bars, benches, tile, doors, flooring, ironwork, statuary, windows, more. Full service restoration company.

Stained Glass

Adkins Architectural Antiques

3515 Fannin St.

Houston, TX 77004

Telephone: 713-522-6547; 800-522-6547

Website: www.adkinsantiques.com

E-mail: adkins@adkinsantiques.com

Antiques, repairs, restorations, custom work; sales and rentals. Hardware, lighting, mantels, plumbing and bath, stained glass, doors, architectural artifacts, weather vanes, garden decor, fountains, odds & ends

Amighini Architectural Inc.

246 Beacon Ave.

Jersey City, NJ 07306

Telephone: 201-222-6367

Fax: 201-222-6368

Website: www.amighini.net

E-mail: info@amighini.net

Imported architectural items from different parts of the world; wholesale also bronze and crystal lighting, stained glass, wooden doors, windows, cupolas, iron pieces, antique tiles, balconies, marble and cast-iron fireplaces, garden accents, panels & fence, more.

Architectural Artifacts, Inc.
4325 Ravenswood
Chicago, IL 60613
Telephone: 773-348-0622
Website: www.architecturalartifacts.com
Period lighting, fireplace mantels, stained glass, doors, tiles, garden furnishings, cast & wrought iron, carved stone, furniture, religious artifacts. No reproductions

Architectural Salvage Warehouse
53 Main St.
Burlington, VT 05401
Telephone: 802-658-5011
Website: www.architecturalsalvagevt.com
E-mail: jon@greatsalvage.com
Hardware, lighting, mantels, plumbing, stained glass, doors, windows, columns, posts, corbels, miscellaneous; we also buy salvage rights to older businesses.

Materials Unlimited
2 West Michigan Ave.
Ypsilanti, MI 48197
Telephone: 800-299-9462
Fax: 734-482-3636
Website: www.materialsunlimited.com
Restored lighting, mantels, stained and beveled glass windows, doors, furniture.

Portland Architectural Salvage
919 Congress St.
Portland, ME 04101
Telephone: 207-780-0634
Website: www.portlandsalvage.com
E-mail: preserve@portlandsalvage.com
Hardware, lighting, mantels, plumbing, stair parts, stained and leaded glass, doors, windows, columns, shutters, furniture, garden items, more.

Sattler's Stained Glass Studio, Ltd.
RR1
Pleasantville, NS B0R 1G0, Canada
Telephone: 902-688-1156
Fax: 902-688-1475
Repair, restoration, conservation, custom stained glass pieces.

Timeless Classic Elegance
3035 Barat Rd.
Montreal, Quebec H3Y 2H6, Canada
Telephone: 514-935-5196
Website: www.timelessclassicelegance.com
E-mail: eserafini@timelessclassicelegance.com
Antique leaded stained glass windows from the UK.

Photo Credits

Dan Mayers: front cover, back cover, 6, 7, 8, 9, 13, 14
top left, 17, 18, 23, 24, 25, 26, 27, 28, 29, 30, 31, 32,
35, 36, 37, 38, 39, 40, 43,44, 45, 46, 49 above and
lower right, 50, 53 upper middle and lower middle,
54 upper, 55, 56, 59, 60, 62, 64, 65, 66, 68, 69, 70,
72, 73, 74-75, 76, 77

H. Weber Wilson: 11; 12; 14 bottom left and right; 15;
16; 19; 20; 21; 22; 49 middle left and right, lower left;
53 upper left and right, lower left and right; 54 lower

William Wright: 10, 71